CAREERS IN THE

RESTAURANT BUSINESS

NOT ALL CAREERS ARE DISTANT abstractions. Careers in law or medicine are worthy goals, for example, but there are many years of school between you and your first successful case or complex surgery. Some careers can be started right now – like many of those in the restaurant industry.

More than five million people work in the restaurant business in the United States, making the prepared foods business one of the largest employers in the country. The restaurant business offers an incredibly wide array of employment opportunities, from servers and bussers, to managers and consultants. That's not even counting the cooks who prepare the food or the chefs who lead them. Careers in cooking are covered in another Careers Report.

The restaurant business is also bursting with opportunities for entrepreneurs looking to start their own business. About 40 percent of all restaurant managers are self-employed. That is an unusually large percentage of self-employed managers in a single industry. Only in the restaurant business are almost half of the industry's leaders working for themselves. If you want to run your own business and you want to get started right now, the restaurant business may be for you.

This is a great time to get into the restaurant business. As more people eat more of their meals away from home, a trend that has been increasing for years, the demand for capable restaurant professionals continues to grow.

WHAT YOU CAN DO NOW

LUCKILY FOR YOU, IT IS EASY TO GET started in the restaurant business. You can get a part-time job in a restaurant. No other industry employs as many young people as the restaurant industry. While it is true that many of the restaurant industry jobs that go to young people are often derisively written off as "McJobs," the reality is that restaurant jobs launch more people into careers than any other kind of work. They may pay only minimum wage and come with few benefits, but these jobs will teach you the importance of simple things like showing up on time and taking responsibility for your own work, and even the work of others. The fast-food giants run some of the best management training programs in the world. You may not think that fast food is your future, but it can be an excellent place to start. You can also look into employment opportunities with full-service restaurants. You will almost certainly start out as a dishwasher or busser (busboy, busgirl, or bus person clears tables, takes dirty dishes to the dishwasher, sets tables, etc.), but you will get an excellent behind-the-scenes view of what it really takes to run a restaurant.

Anyone who wants to carve out a career in the restaurant business should know about cooking. People come to restaurants to eat. They may also come for the atmosphere, prices or location, but food is the main attraction. Take a cooking class. Offer to take on the daily cooking duties at home. Learn your way around the kitchen. Learn how to properly sharpen a knife and fillet a fish. Understand the importance of cleanliness and safety in the kitchen. Even if you do not pursue a career in the kitchen you will still have to work with kitchen staffs, and may even be the manager in charge of making sure they get what they need to do their jobs.

There is no better, faster way to learn about an industry than by reading the trade journals and websites devoted to it. There are many periodicals covering the restaurant business, including *Restaurant Business, Restaurant Startup and Growth, Hotel and Restaurant, Restaurant Magazine, Nation's Restaurant News, QSR Magazine, PMQ Pizza Magazine, Slammed Magazine, Cheers* and *Restaurant Report.*

HISTORY OF THE CAREER

IN ONE FORM OR ANOTHER RESTAURANTS have been around for thousands of years. They have not until recent years been the sophisticated businesses they are today, offering exotic foods within thrilling concepts, and serving entertainment as much as food.

Early restaurants were roadside inns where travelers could get something to eat and even spend the night. The most common travelers were farmers bringing their produce into the city from the country. Such journeys sometimes took a day or two and required making stops along the way. Farmers not only got a decent meal while on the road, they were also able to sell some of their produce to innkeepers where they spent the night.

Restaurants also proliferated in major cities that attracted travelers not in a position to cook for themselves. Even small towns supported an inn or two. These early restaurants, usually known as taverns, inns or pubs were not really restaurants in the modern sense. If you were hungry you ate what was offered that day. There were no public health departments, so there was no quality control.

The word "pub" is just the shortened version of "public house," which is what pubs aimed to be – houses open to the public, complete with living rooms, kitchens and bedrooms. Pubs became more important as commerce grew and more people traveled away from home. Almost nobody traveled for pleasure. Travel was expensive, dangerous and took people away from their families and occupations, both of which needed constant tending.

The very wealthy could afford to have some variety on their table, and they hired creative cooks who turned cooking into an art form. These cooks did not work in public restaurants but rather in castles and palaces. They served hundreds or even thousands of people simultaneously. Their approach to food was the beginning of what we now know as fine dining. Food, presentation, and atmosphere all mattered to these pioneers, but only the lucky few could get a seat at the table.

Many of these culinary pioneers lived in France, long known as the center of culinary arts. They worked for royalty and nobility. Life was good until 1789, when the

French Revolution swept the countryside and did away with the country's aristocracy. Now unemployed, cooks found other ways to ply their trade, including establishing the first restaurants. They catered to an elite clientele of paying customers in their own restaurants. Even the word restaurant is based on the French word "restaurer," which means "to restore."

Restaurants blossomed along with the rise of travel and the need for full-service hotels and eateries. Residents of major cities even started wandering into ethnic neighborhoods to see what was on the menu. It seems hard to believe today but it was only a few decades ago that diners had to go to Italian neighborhoods to get a pizza and to Chinese neighborhoods to get General Tso's chicken.

Two things changed after World War II: women entered the workforce in large numbers, and most people drove cars to go to work and run errands. Americans ate more restaurant meals than ever before, and they needed to be fast and cheap. A salesman named Ray Kroc revolutionized dining forever in the early 1950s, when he sold milkshake machines to the McDonald brothers, who owned a hamburger restaurant in San Bernardino, California. Kroc liked the efficient way the McDonalds went about their business. They kept the menu short so they could get the best price on good ingredients and worked hard to find the simplest, most expeditious way to do everything. Kroc bought franchise rights from the McDonalds in 1954, founded the McDonalds Corporation, and opened the first McDonalds restaurant in 1955 in Des Plaines, Illinois.

Today's restaurant industry is one of the most diverse, exciting industries in the world. Modern transportation and food-storage technology combined with new social attitudes that encourage embracing different cultures have spawned a world of restaurants that was unthinkable only a few decades ago. From fast-food franchises that serve simple, predictable, high-quality food, to fine-dining establishments dabbling in cryogenic cuisine, to enormous resorts that serve thousands of meals a day, the restaurant business has something to offer careerists of all levels and all interests.

WHERE YOU WILL WORK

DO YOU HAVE YOUR SIGHTS SET ON running a restaurant in a resort setting? How about featuring a particular type of regional cuisine? Maybe a franchise? All of these factors and more could determine where you live and work. Resorts tend to be located in places where people want to vacation, like the beach, the mountains, national parks, and theme parks. If you really want to delve into a particular regional cuisine you may have to head to that region, at least at first. Franchise opportunities abound in the restaurant business. Most national brand fast-food restaurants are owned and operated by franchisees – people who pay a fee to a company to use their name and sell their product. Franchisees cannot locate their restaurants just anywhere, however. Usually, they have to choose a location from among those identified by the restaurant's marketing specialists.

Many restaurant professionals spend a few years studying their craft away from home, to learn everything they can at the hands of the masters. France and Italy are popular destinations, as are New York City and the Napa and Sonoma wine regions of Northern California. You may get your start working for major resorts or hotel chains like Disney or Marriott. Some then strike out on their own while others climb the ladder and become senior executives.

DESCRIPTION OF WORK DUTIES

Restaurant Managers

Restaurant managers need to know about everything that happens in a restaurant. Managing a restaurant is an extremely complex job. The list of responsibilities for a typical restaurant manager is extensive: hiring, training, firing, accounting, marketing, advertising, regulatory compliance, purchasing, inventory management, equipment repair, scheduling, customer service, banking, payroll, budgeting, tax compliance, unlocking and turning the lights on, and locking and turning the lights off. Most of these responsibilities could be careers unto themselves. Restaurant managers have to handle them all.

A manager at a full-service restaurant may have one or more assistant managers to help with general management, and an executive chef to manage the kitchen. Managers may also have accountants, lawyers, ad agencies, and equipment technicians on-call to handle very specialized tasks, but the restaurant manager has to supervise everything. Even if an accountant is responsible for keeping the books, for example, the manager is responsible for accumulating and organizing all the information for the accountant. A technician may make the final fix to a malfunctioning dishwasher, but only after the manager figured out how to keep it running to get through a busy Saturday night.

Managers of independent restaurants may be expected to determine their own standards and procedures. Some restaurant owners like to be involved in the day-to-day management of their restaurants, while others hire managers to make most decisions. Managers of franchise restaurants, whether fast-food or table-service, go through a very comprehensive training program and are expected to follow the franchisor's rules on everything from hiring and training, to customer service.

Restaurant managers either rise up through the ranks in the restaurant business, or start out with the skills to put them directly into a management-training program. Many franchisors offer management training to recent college graduates and military veterans, for example. Still, the most common path to the top is by starting at the bottom and doing a little bit of everything. That McJob you got in high school could be your *entrée* – get it? – to leadership in the restaurant business.

Restaurant Owners

Some restaurant owners worked their way up through the business, saved their money, became managers, and eventually opened their own businesses. Others are just wealthy individuals who thought it would be fun to own a restaurant. This report will concentrate on restaurant owners who make it on their own.

Owners may delegate day-to-day responsibility to managers they employ, but owners are ultimately responsible for everything that happens in their restaurant. They also have what is called profit-and-loss responsibility. If the restaurant makes a profit, they get to keep it. If the restaurant loses money, it's their money.

Owners who work their way up through the business may save enough money to start their own place (probably with help from a bank loan), or start a place in partnership with one or more investors. The restaurant business is an excellent business if you want to be your own boss someday. Almost half of all restaurant managers are self-employed, and the entire business, as complex as it is, is geared toward operation by a few people at the top, like managers, executive chefs, and owners.

Servers

In New York and Los Angeles, it is said that there are thousands of restaurant servers "waiting to act." No other profession attracts as many people who would rather be doing something else than waiting tables. Sometimes still known as waiters and waitresses, most such careerists are now known as "server."

The actors and actresses are trying to break into a tough business in which the odds are against them. In the meantime, they have to make a living while still maintaining enough flexibility to go to auditions and short-term acting gigs, like shooting television commercials. Waiting tables offers them exactly the right kind of flexibility. It is also the kind of job that they can give up on a moment's notice when they land a long-term acting job. Done well, and at the right restaurant, waiting tables also pays well. Actors, students, stay-at-home parents who need some extra cash, and many people going through career changes turn to waiting tables to make money.

This is not to say that waiting tables is easy. A busy Saturday night can reduce a newbie to tears. Good servers know their way around the menu so they can make recommendations to customers, always provide flawless customer service no matter what kind of mood they may be in or how badly the customers may be behaving, and never complain. Servers must also be physically fit and maintain a pleasant appearance.

Not everybody passes through waiting tables. Many decide they like the restaurant business, and use their experience waiting on tables to move into cooking or management. Anybody who aspires to be a restaurant manager or owner should spend some time as a server. Servers are usually the only people with whom customers have personal contact when they eat at a restaurant, and customers are ultimately responsible for any restaurant's success.

Bussers

Nobody wants to bus tables for longer than they have to. Bussers clear dishes and clean tables between patrons. This is grunt work. Some restaurants give bussers a cut of the tips received for each shift, but not all do. Bussing tables is a great job while you are still in high school. It's flexible and may come with valuable perks like free meals.

Cooks and Chefs

Many restaurant managers spend some time in the kitchen during their careers. Ultimately, customers choose your restaurant because of the food. If you want to run a restaurant someday you should learn something about what goes on in the kitchen. Spend a year or two as a line cook and you will get a pretty good grip on what it takes to get the food out the door in a timely fashion. On a Friday or Saturday night the kitchens of popular restaurants can be like little war zones. You have to see it to believe it.

Sommeliers and Bartenders

Sommeliers, sometimes known as wine stewards, and bartenders play important roles in many restaurants. Only high-end restaurants employ sommeliers, but even fairly ordinary table-service restaurants employ a skilled bartender or two. Earning sommelier certification takes years of study and a talented palate that you will have to develop. You do not need to become a sommelier in order to put together a solid wine list, however. Becoming a competent bartender is easier than earning sommelier certification but still takes a fair amount of effort. Some high-end restaurants employ full-time beverage managers who hire and train bartenders, buy liquor and wine, and generally run the bar in much the same way the executive chef runs the kitchen.

RESTAURANT PROFESSIONALS TELL THEIR STORIES

I Own a Fine-Dining Restaurant

"Most new restaurants fail within the first five years. I'm one of the lucky ones. I own two fine dining restaurants and they both make money.

I came up in this business the usual way. I started working part time in restaurants while I was in college. I majored in English, which tells you how focused I was on a career – not at all. After graduation, my employer offered to make me the assistant manager of the restaurant where I had been working for four years. Since I had spent time in every department – waiting tables, mixing drinks, cooking and even purchasing ingredients at the local farmers' market – the boss figured I should take on leadership responsibilities since I would be available full time.

As soon as I went full time, I discovered that there is never, ever a dull day in this business. In a typical day I could be called upon to hire a new employee, buy fresh produce, tap a beer keg, fold a hundred napkins, move furniture, take reservations, deal with a health inspector, fix a piece of kitchen equipment, take out the garbage, change light bulbs, mop and vacuum, placate an angry customer, acknowledge compliments from a happy customer, and maybe even help out in the kitchen. To some people this may sound like chaos. To me, it was invigorating.

I managed several restaurants before I started the two places I own now. I had saved money over the years, but I had also made a lot of connections in the restaurant business. When the time came to strike out on my own, I was able to get several investors behind me. Opening a new fine-dining establishment can cost upward of a million dollars. I put up 20 percent of the money and got the rest from passive investors who agreed to let me call most of the shots. I presented them with a concept, a menu, and a business plan. When I had enough investors to make it work, we did the paperwork and off I went.

It took everything I knew from my years of managing other restaurants to stave off disaster. We barely scraped by for the first three years. We worked hard to make a name for ourselves, get good reviews, nurture word-of-mouth referrals for banquets and luncheons, and become a permanent part of the community. I listened to our customers intently. What they wanted, I gave them. I hired and fired a long line of chefs until I found my culinary soul mate, the chef who understood what I wanted and what customers were clamoring for. Finally, it worked. By about the fifth year our revenues evened out, staff turnover slowed down, and we achieved a steady state of profitability.

We found that restaurants that make it past the five-year mark almost always do so because they become a fixture in the community. The people who live and work nearby can't envision the neighborhood without your restaurant in it. You build up a brisk lunch trade with businesspeople in the area, and then dinners with couples and families. You become the go-to place for special occasions like first dates and anniversaries. You only get there by working hard, paying attention and never resting on your laurels.

Since founding that first restaurant I've opened a similar restaurant in a nearby city, and it has also done well. But do you want to know a secret? I also own a small hot-dog place, not far from the first restaurant. It's a typical joint. There are thousands of them all around the metro area. It makes more money than my fine-dining restaurants and requires almost no attention from me. I keep it because it's profitable and because I like hot dogs. I keep the other restaurants because I love the challenges that come with them."

I Am a Server at a Fast-Casual Restaurant

"I'm a philosophy major in college. I need to make money, so I wait tables. I never expected to like it, but now I find myself looking forward to it.

When I started waiting tables I had no experience, but I just knew that waiting tables was the time-honored way to put a few bucks in your pocket on your way to something else. So I got a job at the fast-casual franchise near campus. I didn't like it much at first. The customers seemed so fussy and difficult to me. I quickly discovered that I could usually remedy the situation by making an effort to cater to their needs. It sounds like simple customer service logic, but I had never thought about it before. It didn't take long for me to figure out that the key to the whole interaction is to make the customer happy.

That's what I like best about being a server. Most part-time jobs pay a flat wage and they don't pay very well. Most of my income comes from tips, and I can control how big they are by providing excellent service. Most people like to reward superior service, so I give it to them. I make more money than I could doing any other part-time job, and I enjoy it.

I don't know if I'll stay in this business for the long haul. Having my degree could get me into a management-training program at my restaurant or one like it. The hours can be challenging but I like the people I work with, and they have the same crazy hours I do. I plan to take a hard look at this business after I graduate."

I Manage a Fast-food Franchise

"I started working for this company when I was 16. I kept the job on a part-time basis all the way through high school. After graduation I went full time and earned an associate degree in food service management. I also went through my company's rigorous management training program.

Running a franchise restaurant means doing everything by the book. The company has rules and procedures for everything you can imagine. They have been honed over the course of many decades. We are famous for our customer service, and for the opportunities presented by our tendency to promote from within whenever possible. We work very hard at both of these things. One keeps the customers happy, the other keeps the employees happy.

The hardest part of my job, by far, is managing the workforce. We employ a lot of young people. Many teenagers haven't figured out why it's important to be on time, or why they need to get a haircut once in a while, or why it's never acceptable to argue with a customer. Most of them figure it out, but not all of them do. I fire a lot of people. Most of the people I fire are not raising families and paying bills, however. They're kids who need a few life lessons on their way up.

I would recommend this job to anybody who likes a fast-paced environment and a lot of variety. I don't think I could stand being stuck behind a desk doing the same thing all day long. I even like the occasional crisis. If the idea of a small fire in the kitchen terrifies you, stay far away from the restaurant business."

I Am a Manager at a Full-Service Franchise

"I've loved the restaurant business for as long as I can remember. When I was a kid, nothing excited me as much as going out to eat with my parents. It was exciting to go to restaurants with interesting themes and have people bring me cool food I never got at home. I've never lost that fascination with restaurants. It came as no surprise when I decided to major in restaurant management in college. I had been working in restaurants since I was a teenager, from fast-food franchises to nice fast-casual places, and I was a pretty good cook in my own right. I wanted to pull it all together with a proper training program, so off I went to restaurant and hospitality school.

Restaurant management is a very hands-on business, so I spent much of my time in college doing things, as opposed to reading about them. My college had a rigorous general-education requirement, so it was not like I was just taking fun classes. I had to take the same basic English, math, history and science courses everybody else has to take. A broad liberal-arts education is a good thing to have.

My favorite part of college, by far, was the six-month internship I completed at a famous resort in Florida. It was usually a one-semester internship but they let me stick around for summer vacation and keep working at the resort. The resort is huge, and I learned a little about all of the things they have going on there. Some people make a career out of working there, and I can see why.

After college, I wanted to get out into the business and learn everything I could. I was recruited by a major upscale franchise and invited to go through their management-training program. The whole program lasts a year and is composed of classroom and on-the-job training. About half of those who start the program don't make it to the end. This is a high-end, expensive restaurant. A single franchise costs millions of dollars and there aren't very many of them.

My employer specializes in steak. We have a pretty limited menu of steakhouse favorites including, obviously, steak, lobster tail, prime cuts of fish, wedge salads, baked potatoes and fabulous desserts. Lots of restaurants offer similar menus but few do it as well as we do it. We source our steaks directly from cattle ranches in Oklahoma and Texas, for example. Our bleu cheese dressing is mostly bleu cheese, which isn't cheap. Our lobster tails are all attached to lobsters when we get them, and the lobsters are alive. You have no idea how many kinds of potatoes there are until you have worked here. We get the best. A couple on a date cannot get out of here for less than $150. This is the kind of place where you go to splurge.

I don't know where this career might take me. I'm still pretty young. I could stay with this employer for a long time. After I've been here for a few more years, however, it wouldn't be hard to try somewhere new. I could even go back to that resort in Florida and run one of their high-end restaurants. For now, I'm very happy where I am."

PERSONAL QUALIFICATIONS

CAREERS IN THE RESTAURANT BUSINESS can be very challenging. Most people would not last very long without a few important personal qualities. To succeed you must have an excellent head for business. Restaurants can fall victim to any number of threats almost overnight. To succeed you can never forget that a restaurant is a business. This means paying careful attention to the bottom line. The basic formula for financial success in the restaurant business is to spend one third of your money on labor, one third on food, and one third on everything else. Deviating from this formula could have very negative consequences. Many restaurateurs try to pinch pennies by using cheap ingredients, cutting back on wait staff or putting off maintenance on their buildings, thinking that customers won't notice. Customers always notice, and when they do, they don't come back. Without customers you have nothing but an empty space. All businesses are customer-driven, but some are more personal than others. Restaurants supply much more than just food. They provide food, entertainment, conviviality, and a complex experience that can be derailed by the tiniest mistake. Some people will not come back if their food was not perfect. Others refuse to return because the music was too loud. Still others balk at prices that are higher than they think they should be. Rude service will turn just about anybody away. Providing excellent customer service requires a singular blend of pride and humility that can be hard for some people to muster. Humility because excellent customer service is never about you, and pride because giving the customers what they want is something to be proud of.

If your goal is to make it into the managerial ranks you also need to be a good leader. Some people use the words "lead" and "manage" interchangeably. Managers – the catch-all term for people who have authority over others – lead people and manage projects. You may make a pretty good project manager if all you have to do is move data around on a spreadsheet. Leading people requires another skill. Much has been written about leadership, and nobody has the definitive answer about what works best in all situations. Leadership is much more of an art than a science, and it requires a deft touch by leaders who care about their people and their mission. Leadership is also a skill that is mostly learned in the field. If you have leadership potential, you probably know it already.

ATTRACTIVE ASPECTS

CAREERS IN THE RESTAURANT BUSINESS are wide open to innovation. Entrepreneurship is common throughout the business, from fast-food joints to fine-dining establishments.

It is an absolute truism that the toughest jobs are also the most satisfying. Many people think of the restaurant business as grunt work for people who cannot do anything else, or for those who are on their way to something better. Nothing could be further from the truth. People eat out to have an experience. Giving them a memorable one is not easy. If you enter this profession, you will find that the best restaurateurs are driven, creative and extremely resourceful. They love their careers and probably wouldn't want to do anything else.

Part of the reason that restaurateurs love their careers is that they are so open to innovation. Chefs apply their creativity to the food, but managers apply their creativity to everything else. Famous chains like the Hard Rock Café succeed not because of the food – which is perfectly good though equally ordinary – but because of the experience that comes with the food. All those guitars autographed by famous rock stars are pretty cool. The same goes for restaurants with great views or restaurants with a gimmick, like slowly revolving atop a hotel or dressing up their interior with an over-the-top theme. Restaurateurs who have relatively little to do with food can craft singular experiences that will keep diners coming back. The number of details that can be tweaked or improved is immense. Seating, tables, colors, linens, and lighting are just a few of the elements that contribute to the experience of dining at a particular restaurant. There are interior designers and architects, for example, who specialize in restaurants. Their expertise can be critical to the success or failure of a restaurant. Like the best leaders in any business, the best restaurateurs surround themselves with capable, creative people who can help the business to succeed. If you get into this business you will have innumerable opportunities to follow your vision.

This is especially true if you want to own your own restaurant someday. About 40 percent of restaurant managers are self-employed. To say that is a high number would be an understatement. You would have to look hard to find another profession in which self-employment is so common. Not only is self-employment common, there are even different types of self-employment. Owning your own restaurant is the obvious type of self-employment. Restaurateurs who start their own restaurants spend years working for somebody else first. There is too much to learn to start your own restaurant without significant experience, even if fate dropped the investment money in your lap.

Many restaurateurs own franchises of popular restaurant chains. McDonald's is by far the largest such franchise company, followed by Subway and Burger King. Many table-service restaurants are also franchises, including Applebee's, Ruby Tuesday, and fine-dining stalwart Ruth's Chris. Franchises come with many advantages. Franchise fees can be expensive, but after you get one you also get support from the head office, training for you and your staff, and automatic inclusion in advertising and marketing campaigns. Mostly you get a well-known brand that you don't have to build yourself. The downside, of course, is that you have to stick to the franchisor's rules. McDonald's Big Mac sandwich was created by a Pittsburgh franchisee who sold the idea to the head office, rather than the other way around.

UNATTRACTIVE FEATURES

OPPORTUNITIES FOR INNOVATION AND entrepreneurship aside, the restaurant business has negative aspects. By now you have probably noted that this is a very hard business to succeed in.

Statistics vary, but it is safe to say that about 75 percent of restaurants fail within five years of opening. That means that three quarters of all entrepreneurial efforts, three quarters of all new ideas, and three quarters of all capital invested in new restaurants fails to make a lasting impression on the public. It is not quite go-to-Hollywood-to-make-it-big rough, but the odds are definitely not in your favor. There are numerous reasons for this failure rate. Chief among them are failing to offer a unique experience to customers, and failing to recognize that good food alone is not enough to guarantee a restaurant's success.

If you go into this business you should remind yourself each and every day to pay close attention to the details. You need to be on top of everything, all the time. Surprises are bad. You will have to become a jack-of-all-trades and know more than a little about leadership, management, public health, cooking, customer service, accounting, marketing, carpentry, plumbing, commercial laundry, and many, many more aspects. Any errors or missteps can be fatal to your business. You will need to be a multitasking wizard just to keep your head above water.

The restaurant business comes with what are commonly known as antisocial hours. That is, you will work when everybody else has time off. Forget about Saturday night with your significant other. You will work every Friday and Saturday night for the duration of your career. Your days off are likely to be Monday and maybe Tuesday. You may be able to take off for holidays that are known for gathering with family at home, like Thanksgiving and Christmas, but you can forget about holidays devoted to partying with friends. New Year's Eve, Independence Day, Memorial Day, Labor Day and quasi-holidays like Halloween and St. Patrick's Day will be workdays for you, and probably long ones at that. This may seem like a minor problem today, but when you have a spouse and children operating on a regular schedule, it could become a major issue. Antisocial hours are one of the major reasons people get out of the restaurant business.

No matter how well you succeed in the restaurant business, there will always be those who think of you as a semi-skilled laborer who does work nobody else wants to do. They are wrong, but it is not hard to figure out where they get their impressions. Entry-level jobs in the restaurant business are at the bottom rung of the socioeconomic ladder. They pay poorly and come with few, if any, benefits. They often involve unpleasant tasks like washing dishes or cleaning restrooms. Nobody really wants these jobs. People take them because they need the money or because they are passing through on their way to something better. Some of those people decide they like the restaurant business. They climb the ladder. Along the way they learn the countless details that make the restaurant business go. They become the best managers in the business. Do not let the negative stereotype stop you from starting a career in restaurants.

EDUCATION AND TRAINING

YOU DO NOT NEED TO EARN A degree in order to get into the restaurant business. You do not even need a high school diploma. Many restaurant professionals get their start while they are still in high school and simply grow their careers as they gain more experience. Some never pursue formal education and still manage to do pretty well. In an industry in which so many people work for themselves it should come as no surprise that some people see little value in earning credentials.

There is no question, however, that the straightest path to the top includes formal education at the college level, a path no different from most complex professions. An associate degree in restaurant management or hospitality management should be considered a necessity, and a bachelor's degree is better. Many schools offer comprehensive programs that cover all aspects of the restaurant business, including accounting, marketing, restaurant and kitchen design, wine selection, cooking, hospitality business law, human resources and personnel management, and customer service. Degree programs also come with general education requirements for subjects like English, math, history, and science, just like any other degree program.

There are also many culinary programs to choose from that specialize in cooking, usually geared toward careers as a chef or pastry maker. Many cooks eventually slide into restaurant management after a few years as chefs. Many people think "chef" is a title bestowed upon an excellent cook, but there is more to it. Chefs are leaders and managers. Senior cooks who prove they have leadership ability are promoted to chef. They may also be excellent cooks, but the title refers to their position as leaders.

Earning a degree says very clearly that you want to be in the restaurant business. You are not passing through, and you take the business very seriously. You want to get ahead and are dedicated to making a career out of this challenging industry. Some restaurateurs go on to earn master's degrees in restaurant or hospitality management, especially if they work for very large organizations that offer senior executive opportunities. You can cross that bridge when you get there.

There are two opportunities you must take advantage of while you are in college: an internship and the chance to study abroad. An internship, simply stated, is a job related to your major field of study that takes the place of classes for a summer or semester. Most internships are paid, and many come with opportunities not available to regular employees, like special seminars and tours. An internship is an opportunity to work alongside professionals in the field you think you want to enter. Some days you may be given serious responsibilities, other days you may be making coffee for the boss. No matter what, you will learn just by being in the room with actual professionals for five days a week. Never again will you have the opportunity to try on a career for a few months and then walk away without burning your bridges behind you. Given the fact that you want to enter the restaurant business you should set your sights on an internship doing something big, like working at a tropical resort in Florida or a major hotel in New York City. Disney hires thousands of interns every year to work at Walt Disney World in Florida, and many of those interns work in the company's enormous food service operation. The possibilities are endless. Do not let this opportunity pass you by.

Studying abroad will open your mind in a way that no other experience can. Not everybody thinks the way Americans do, not even in other developed countries. Spending a few months or even an entire academic year studying in a foreign country will change your life. As an aspiring restaurant professional, you will learn invaluable lessons by getting to know another culture's cuisine. You will also learn about how they run restaurants and what they expect from customer-service providers. This can be very eye opening. With some effort, you may be able to find a study-abroad experience that includes paid work, which is even better. Do not let this opportunity pass you by either.

EARNINGS

EARNINGS IN THE RESTAURANT BUSINESS are what you make of them. Historically, the restaurant business has been associated with lower-level jobs that pay little and are usually a stepping stone to something else. On the other hand, the profusion in recent years of television programs about the adventures of restaurant owners and celebrity chefs could lead one to believe that the restaurant business is a glamorous high-earnings profession.

For the vast majority of restaurant professionals the truth lies somewhere in-between. At any given time there are millions of people working in the restaurant business for minimum wages because they need jobs, not because they have any intention of staying in the restaurant business. Most of those people leave the business in a year or two and create opportunities for other people to make ends meet, while they pursue whatever it is they really want to do. This is basically a good thing. The restaurant business provides flexible, short-term employment to people who need it.

Some of those people, however, decide they like the business and start to climb the ladder. Others, like you, choose to enter the restaurant business because it is an interesting, challenging way to earn a living. Even you may have to start on the bottom rung. You probably will not stay there very long. Restaurant managers have experience separating those who like the business and want to make it a lifetime career from those who only want to do it for a short while. Prove that you want to be in the business and you will move up in the world pretty quickly.

Many restaurant business jobs pay the minimum wage. Minimum wage varies by jurisdiction, but as of this writing the federal minimum wage is $7.25 per hour. Many states require higher minimum wages. Some states allow people working in traditionally tipped professions to be paid less than minimum wage on the assumption that most of their income will come from tips. This is definitely true for wait staff, and even for bussers who are entitled to a share of the tips at the end of the shift. It is common for wait staff in table-service restaurants to earn at least $100 per shift and more on busy dinner shifts. Given scheduling flexibility full-time wait staff can earn $25,000 per year fairly easily, and potentially much more if they work for fine-dining establishments and provide exceptional service.

Restaurant managers can earn anywhere from $35,000 per year if they start their careers in fast food or fast-casual, to more like $65,000 to $85,000 per year as they gain seniority and experience. The sky is the limit if you open your own restaurant. You could make a million or, lose a million.

OPPORTUNITIES

THE RESTAURANT BUSINESS IS ARGUABLY unequaled in the sheer number of ways you can move up in the world. Any business in which nearly half of the leaders are self-employed obviously recognizes innovation. Paying close attention to the dollars and cents will never hurt your career. Neither will earning a new credential once in a while.

Never be afraid to stick your neck out in the restaurant business. Given the fact that most restaurants go belly up in a short time, you really have nothing to lose. Experiment. Take risks. Come up with the Next Big Thing. You will not always get it right, but so what? You will be in good company when it goes wrong. Then you can try again. Restaurateurs like to talk about concepts. Every new restaurant has to have a concept. There are rules to follow but rules also need to be broken in order to come up with something truly new. Consumers are funny that way. They want their reliable favorites, but they are constantly on the hunt for something new and different. Sociologists study this behavior, and you should too. Spend a few years learning the business from somebody else and then, when you are ready, strike out on your own. Maybe with a partner or two. You will find no business friendlier to entrepreneurship.

No matter how creative your concept, you can never forget that running a restaurant is a business. Let yourself dream big dreams but do not become beholden to them. The best restaurateurs know exactly how many napkins they have in stock at any given time. They can tell you when they bought their vegetables and exactly what the sell-by dates are on the dairy products in the refrigerator. They know how much electricity, water, and gas they use. They are definitely on top of labor costs and pay attention to what advertising works and what does not. They can probably fix their own websites, too. If your goal is to move up in the world you will not score any points by wasting money. This is as true for wait staff as it is for managers. Prove yourself to be a good businessperson and you will be rewarded.

All professions require credentials of some sort. The restaurant business is no different. Even if you have already earned a degree in restaurant management or hospitality, you should seize opportunities to earn professional certificates in related disciplines. Many restaurant managers earn professional certification in wine buying and tasting, for example. Such a certificate does not make them full-fledged sommeliers but can definitely be helpful when the time comes to buy wines for a new season or even when making a recommendation to a customer. Restaurateurs also need to stay current on health and labor certifications, which vary from one jurisdiction to the next. Always be willing to beef up your résumé.

GETTING STARTED

GIVEN THE RESTAURANT BUSINESS'S flexible nature and the wide variety of jobs available to young people there is no reason you should not already have a restaurant job by the time you finish school. The trick is getting that first big job that will launch your career. Get in touch with all of the contacts you have made over the years and see what they have to offer.

If you already had a few restaurant jobs, a college internship and a few credentials you should have a pretty sizeable list of connections in the business. So contact them and pick their brains a bit. It is very common for recent college graduates to get their first professional job from an employer who already knows them, whether from a part-time job or an internship. As someone who already understands the culture and procedures of the restaurant, you are a sure thing and can be hired quickly and efficiently, skipping the expensive and time-consuming process of advertising and interviewing. So take advantage of your connections. Even if the people you know do not have anything right away, they may know of somebody who does. It never hurts to ask.

Even restaurateurs need résumés. Take the time to get your résumé right. Most résumés are looked at for only about 10 seconds before they go into the trash or into the small pile of applicants who will be called for interviews. There is no shortage of books and software applications that can help you to craft an excellent résumé. There are also professional résumé-writers who can make you look better than you ever thought possible. Although many professions mostly use online applications that do not require a traditional paper résumé, the restaurant business is still characterized by relatively small operations and hands-on management. You will almost certainly have to hand over a few paper résumés during your job hunt. It behooves you to put your best foot forward.

As you head out into the real world do not lose sight of the fact that you are just getting started. You do not need to land your dream job the first time out. In fact, you probably will not even know what your dream job is. It could take a decade or more before you really zero in on the thing that makes you happiest. Everything you learn now will help you to fine-tune your goals and home in on your dream job later in your career. Open your mind, take a few risks, and dive in. Good luck.

ASSOCIATIONS, PERIODICALS, WEBSITES

■ **American Restaurant Association**
www.americanrestaurantassociation.com

■ **Art Institutes**
www.go.artinstitutes.edu

■ **California Polytechnic Institute Pomona**
www.cpp.edu

■ **California Restaurant Association**
www.calrest.org

■ **Cheers**
www.cheersonline.com

■ **Cornell University**
www.cornell.edu

■ **Culinary Institute of America**
www.ciachef.edu

■ **Disney**
www.disney.com

■ **Drexel University**
www.drexel.edu

■ **Florida Restaurant and Lodging Association**
www.frla.org

■ **Hilton**
www.hilton.com

■ **Hospitality Careers**
www.hcareers.com

■ **Hospitality Online**
www.hospitalityonline.com

■ **Hotel and Restaurant Magazine**
www.hotelfandb.com

■ **Illinois Restaurant Association**
www.illinoisrestaurants.org

■ **Johnson and Wales University**
www.jwu.edu

■ **Kendall College**
www.kendall.edu

■ **Le Cordon Bleu**
www.national.chefs.edu

■ **Marriott**
www.marriott.com

■ **National Restaurant Association**
www.restaurant.org

■ **Nation's Restaurant News**
www.nrn.com

■ **New York State Restaurant Association**
www.nysra.org

■ **PMQ Pizza Magazine**
www.pmq.com

■ **Purdue University**
www.purdue.edu

■ **QSR Magazine**
www.qsrmagazine.com

■ **Restaurant Business Magazine**
www.restaurantbusinessonline.com

■ **Restaurant Report**
www.restaurantreport.com

■ **Restaurant Startup and Growth**
www.rsgmag.com

■ **ServSafe**
www.servsafe.com

■ **Slammed Magazine**
www.slammedmagazine.com

■ **Starwood Hotels and Resorts**
www.starwoodhotels.com

■ **University of Central Florida**
www.ucf.edu

■ **University of Houston**
www.uh.edu

■ **University of Nevada Las Vegas**
www.unlv.edu

■ **University of Pennsylvania**
www.upenn.edu

www.ingramcontent.com/pod-product-compliance
Lightning Source LLC
Chambersburg PA
CBHW072315200526
45168CB00014B/1601